Palo Alto ACE - Accredited Configuration Engineer Exam Practice Questions & Dumps

Exam Practice Questions for Palo Alto ACE Exam Prep
LATEST VERSION

PRESENTED BY: Quantic Books

About Quantic Books:

Quantic Books is a publishing house based in Princeton, New Jersey, USA. , a platform that is accessible online as well as locally, which gives power to educational content, erudite collection, poetry & many other book genres. We make it easy for writers & authors to get their books designed, published, promoted, and sell professionally on worldwide scale with eBook + Print distribution. Quantic Books is now distributing books worldwide.

Note: Find answers of the questions at the last of the book.

QUESTION 1

Once the setting up of a latest version of PANOS, the firewall should be rebooted.

A. Correct
B. Incorrect

QUESTION 2

When configuring a Decryption Policy Regulation, which of the given are accessible as corresponding conditions in the regulation? (Select three.)

A. Source Zone
B. URL Group
C. Application
D. Service
E. Source User

QUESTION 3

What is the purpose of the GlobalProtect Portal?

A. To sustain the list of Global Protect Gateways and necessitate HIP data that the agent must report.
B. To loadbalance
C. GlobalProtect customer connections to GlobalProtect Gateways.
D. To sustain the list of remote GlobalProtect Portals and the list of groups for certifying the customer machine.
E. To give dismissal for tunneled connections through the GlobalProtect Gateways.

QUESTION 4

Which mode will permit a user to select when they wish to connect to the Global Protect Network?

A. Always On mode
B. Choiceal mode
C. Single SignOn mode
D. On Demand mode

QUESTION 5

Once the installation of a latest Application and Threat database, the firewall should be rebooted.

A. Correct
B. Incorrect

QUESTION 6

Considering only the data in the snapshot above, answer the given question: A span port or a switch is connected to e1/4, but there are no traffic logs.
Which of the given conditions most expectedly clarifies this behavior?

A. The interface is not given a virtual router.
B. The interface is not given an IP address.
C. The interface is not up.
D. There is no zone given to the interface.

QUESTION 7

Which of the given platforms supports the Decryption Port
Mirror task?

A. PA3000
B. VMSeries 100
C. PA2000
D. PA4000

QUESTION 8

UserID is facilitated in the configuration of:

A. a Security Profile.
B. an Interface.
C. a Security Policy.
D. a Zone.

QUESTION 9

Which of the given interface kinds can have an IP address
given to it?

A. Layer 3
B. Layer 2
C. Tap
D. Virtual Wire

QUESTION 10

As the Palo Alto Networks Administrator you have facilitated Application Block pages.
later, not recognizing they are trying to access a blocked web based application, users call the Help Desk to make a complaint regarding network connectivity problems. What is the basis of the augmented number of help desk calls?

A. The File Blocking Block Page was deactivated.
B. Some AppID's are set with a Session Timeout value that is too low.
C. The firewall admin did not make a custom response page to inform possible users that their effort to access the web based application is being blocked as it should be to policy.
D. Application Block Pages will only be displayed when Captive Portal is configured.

QUESTION 11

Security policies necessitate a source interface and a destination interface.

A. Correct
B. Incorrect

QUESTION 12

Select the implicit regulations that are functional to traffic that fails to match any administrator defined Security Policies.

A. Intrazone traffic is permitted
B. Interzone traffic is denied
C. Intrazone traffic is denied
D. Interzone traffic is permitted

QUESTION 13

Besides choosing the Heartbeat Backup choice when making an ActivePassive HA Pair, which of the given also avoids "SplitBrain"?

A. Making a custom interface under Service Route Configuration, and assigning this interface as the backup HA2 link.
B. Under "Packet Forwarding", choosing the VR Sync checkbox.
C. Configuring an independent backup HA1 link.
D. Configuring a backup HA2 link that points to the MGT interface of the other device in the pair.

QUESTION 14

Which of the given reports is NOT Correct regarding a Decryption Mirror interface?

A. Needs superuser privilege
B. Supports SSL outbound
C. Can be a member of any VSYS
D. Supports SSL inbound

QUESTION 15

Which of the given particulars regarding dynamic updates is accurate?

A. Antivirus updates are released daily. Application and Threat updates are released weekly.
B. Application and Antivirus updates are released weekly. Threat and "Threat and URL Filtering" updates are released weekly.
C. Application and Threat updates are released daily. Antivirus and URL Filtering updates are released weekly.
D. Threat and URL Filtering updates are released daily. Application and Antivirus updates are released weekly.

QUESTION 16

"What is the result of an Administrator submitting a WildFire report's verdict back to Palo Alto Networks as "Inaccurate"?

A. The signature will be updated for Incorrect positive and Incorrect negative files in the next AV signature update.
B. The signature will be updated for Incorrect positive and Incorrect negative files in the next Application signature update.
C. You will accept an email to deactivate the signature manually.
D. You will accept an update within 15 minutes.

QUESTION 17

When configuring the firewall for UserID, what is the extreme number of Domain Controllers that can be configured?

A. 100
B. 50
C. 10
D. 150

QUESTION 18

In a Palo Alto Networks firewall, every interface in use should be given to a zone in order to process traffic.

A. Correct
B. Incorrect

QUESTION 19

Considering only the data in the snapshot above, answer the given question. An administrator is pinging 4.4.4.4 and fails to accept a response. What is the most expectedly reason for the absence of response?

A. The interface is down.
B. There is a Security Policy that avoids ping.
C. There is no Management Profile.
D. There is no route back to the machine originating the ping.

QUESTION 20

Which type of license is needed to perform Decryption Port Mirroring?

A. A free PANPADecrypt license
B. A subscriptionbased
C. SSL Port license
D. A Customer Decryption license
E. A subscriptionbased PANPADecrypt license

QUESTION 21

In which of the given can UserID be used to offer a match condition?

A. Security Policies
B. NAT Policies
C. Zone Protection Policies
D. Threat Profiles

QUESTION 22

Which of the given are essential elements of a GlobalProtect solution?
A. GlobalProtect Gateway, GlobalProtect Agent, GlobalProtect Portal
B. GlobalProtect Gateway, GlobalProtect Agent, GlobalProtect Server
C. GlobalProtect Gateway, GlobalProtect NetConnect, GlobalProtect Agent, GlobalProtect Portal, GlobalProtect Server
D. GlobalProtect NetConnect, GlobalProtect Agent, GlobalProtect Portal, GlobalProtect Server

QUESTION 23

Which attribute can be configured to block sessions that the firewall cannot decrypt?

A. Decryption Profile in Decryption Policy
B. Decryption Profile in Security Profile
C. Decryption Profile in PBF
D. Decryption Profile in Security Policy

QUESTION 24

How do you reduce the amount of data recorded in the URL Content Filtering Logs?

A. Activate "Log container page only".
B. Deactivate URL packet captures.
C. Activate URL log caching.
D. Activate DSRI.

QUESTION 25

Considering only the data in the snapshot above, answer the given question. An administrator is using SSH on port 3333 and BitTorrent on port 7777. Which reports are correct?

A. The BitTorrent traffic will be permitted.
B. The SSH traffic will be permitted.
C. The SSH traffic will be denied.
D. The BitTorrent traffic will be denied.

QUESTION 26

Which of the given reports is NOT Correct about Palo Alto Networks firewalls?

A. The Admin account may be deactivated.
B. System defaults may be restored by performing a factory reset in Maintenance Mode.
C. The Admin account may not be deactivated.
D. Initial configuration may be accomplished thru the MGT interface or the Console port.

QUESTION 27

When using remote verification for users (LDAP, RADIUS, Active Directory, etc.), what should be done to permit a user to authenticate through numerous procedures?

A. Make an Verification Sequence, dictating the order of verification profiles.
B. Make numerous verification profiles for the same user.
C. This cannot be done. A single user can only use one verification type.
D. This cannot be done. Although numerous verification procedures exist, a firewall should select a single, global verification type and all users should use this procedure.

QUESTION 28

If the Forward Proxy Ready shows "no" when running the command show system setting ssl-decrypt setting, what is most expectedly the basis?

A. SSL forward proxy certificate is not generated
B. Web interface certificate is not generated
C. Forward proxy license is not facilitated on the box n
D. SSL decryption regulation is not formed

QUESTION 29

When adding an application in a Policy-based Forwarding regulation, only a subset of the entire App-ID database is represented. Why would this be?

A. Policy-based forwarding can only indentify certain applications at this stage of the packet flow, as the majority of applications are only identified once the session is formed.
B. Policy-based forwarding regulations necessitate that a companion Security policy regulation, letting the needed Application traffic, should first be formed.
C. The license for the Application ID database is no longer valid.
D. A custom application should first be defined before it can be added to a Policy-based forwarding regulation.

QUESTION 30
What choice must be configured when using User ID?

A. Activate User ID per Zone
B. Activate User ID per Security Regulation
C. Activate User ID per interface
D. None of the above

QUESTION 31

What needs to be done prior to committing a configuration in Panorama once making a change via the CLI or web interface on a device?

A. No additional actions needed
B. Synchronize the configuration amid the device and Panorama
C. Make the same change again via Panorama
D. Re-import the configuration from the device into Panorama

QUESTION 32

Which local interface cannot be given to the IKE gateway?

A. Tunnel
B. L3
C. VLAN
D. Loopback

QUESTION 33

To permit the PAN device to resolve internal and external DNS host names for reporting and for security policies, an administrator can do the given:

A. Make a DNS Proxy Object with a default DNS Server for external resolution and a DNS server for internal domain. Then, in the device settings, point to this proxy object for DNS resolution.
B. In the device settings define internal hosts via a static list.
C. In the device settings set the Primary DNS server to an external server and the secondary to an internal server.
D. Make a DNS Proxy Object with a default DNS Server for external resolution and a DNS server for internal domain. Then, in the device settings, select the proxy object as the Primary DNS and make a custom security regulation which references that object for

QUESTION 34

With PAN-OS 5.0, how can a common NTP value be pushed to a cluster of firewalls?

A. Via a Panorama Template
B. Via a shared object in Panorama
C. Via a Panorama Device Group
D. Via a Device Group object in Panorama

QUESTION 35

Which of the given Global Protect attribute s needs a separate license?

A. Use of dynamic selection amid numerous Gateways
B. Use of a Portal to permit users to connect
C. Letting users to connect
D. Manual Gateway Selection

QUESTION 36

Which of the given represents HTTP traffic events that can be used to identify possible Botnets?

A. Traffic from users that browse to IP addresses instead of fully-qualified domain names, downloading W32.Welchia.Worm from a Windows share, traffic to domains that have been registered in the last 30 days, downloading executable files from unknown URL's
B. Traffic from users that browse to IP addresses instead of fully-qualified domain names, traffic to domains that have been registered in the last 60 days, downloading executable files from unknown URL's
C. Traffic from users that browse to IP addresses instead of fully-qualified domain names, traffic to domains that have been registered in the last 60 days, downloading executable files from unknown URL's, IRC-based Command and Control traffic
D. Traffic from users that browse to IP addresses instead of fully-qualified domain names, traffic to domains that have been registered in the last 30 days.

QUESTION 37

For accurate routing to SSL VPN customers to occur, the given should be configured:

A. Network Address Translation should be facilitated for the SSL VPN customer IP pool
B. A dynamic routing protocol amid the Palo Alto Networks device and the next-hop gateway to advertise the SSL VPN customer IP pool
C. A static route on the next-hop gateway of the SSL VPN customer IP pool with a destination of the Palo Alto Networks device
D. No routing needs to be configured - the PAN device automatically responds to ARP requests for the SSL VPN customer IP pool

QUESTION 38

Which choice lets an administrator to segrate Panorama and Syslog traffic, so that the Management Interface is not employed when sending these kinds of traffic?

A. Custom entries in the Virtual Router, pointing to the IP addresses of the Panorama and Syslog devices.
B. Define a Loopback interface for the Panorama and Syslog Devices
C. On the Device tab in the Web UI, make custom server profiles for Syslog and Panorama
D. Service Route Configuration

QUESTION 39

What latest functionality is given in PAN-OS 5.0 by Palo Alto Networks URL Filtering Database (PAN-DB)?

A. The "Log Container Page Only" choice can be employed in a URL-Filtering policy to reduce the number of logging events.
B. URL-Filtering can now be employed as a match condition in Security policy
C. IP-Based Threat Exceptions can now be driven by custom URL groups
D. Daily database downloads for updates are no longer needed as devices stay in-sync with the cloud.

QUESTION 40

For non-Microsoft customers, what Captive Portal procedure is supported?

A. NTLM Auth
B. User Agent
C. Local Database
D. Web Form Captive Portal

QUESTION 41

In order to route traffic amid layer 3 interfaces on the PAN firewall you need:

A. VLAN
B. Vwire
C. Security Profile
D. Virtual Router

QUESTION 42

What built-in administrator role lets all rights except for the creation of administrative accounts and virtual systems?

A. superuser
B. vsysadmin
C. A custom role is needed for this level of access
D. Deviceadmin

QUESTION 43

What is the name of the debug save file for IPSec VPN tunnels?

A. set vpn all up
B. test vpn ike-sa
C. request vpn IPsec-sa test
D. Ikemgr.pcap

QUESTION 44

To make a custom signature object for an Application Override Policy, which of the given fields are mandatory?

A. Group
B. Regular Expressions
C. Ports
D. Characteristics

QUESTION 45

Which routing protocol is supported on the Palo Alto Networks platform?

A. BGP
B. RSTP
C. ISIS
D. RIPv1

QUESTION 46

What happens at the point of Threat Prevention license expiration?

A. Threat Prevention no longer updated; existing database still effective
B. Threat Prevention is no longer used; applicable traffic is permitted
C. Threat Prevention no longer used; applicable traffic is blocked
D. Threat Prevention no longer used; traffic is permitted or blocked by configuration per Security Regulation

QUESTION 47

Administrative Alarms can be facilitated for which of the given except?

A. Certificate Expirations
B. Security Violation Thresholds
C. Security Policy Tags
D. Traffic Log capacity

QUESTION 48

As the Palo Alto Networks administrator responsible for User ID, you are looking for the simplest procedure of mapping network users that do not sign into LDAP. Which data source would permit reliable User ID mapping for these users, requiring the least amount of configuration?

A. WMI Query
B. Exchange CAS Security Logs
C. Captive Portal
D. Active Directory Security Logs

QUESTION 49

Which mode will permit a user to select how they wish to connect to the GlobalProtect Network as they would like?

A. Single Sign-On Mode
B. On Demand Mode
C. Always On Mode
D. Choiceal Mode

QUESTION 50

Which of the given should be configured when deploying User-ID to obtain data from an 802.1x authenticator?

A. Terminal Server Agent
B. An Agentless deployment of User-ID, employing only the Palo Alto Networks Firewall
C. A User-ID agent, with the "Use for NTLM Verification" choice facilitated.
D. XML API for User-ID Agent

QUESTION 51

Which of the given choices may be facilitated to reduce system overhead when using Content ID?

A. STP
B. VRRP
C. RSTP
D. DSRI

QUESTION 52

When making an application filter, which of the given is correct?

A. They are used by malware
B. Excessive bandwidth may be used as a filter match conditions
C. They are called dynamic for the reason that they automatically adapt to latest IP addresses
D. They are called dynamic for the reason that they will automatically include latest applications from an application signature update if the latest application's type is included in the filter

QUESTION 53

Which fields can be altered in the default Vulnerability profile?

A. Severity
B. Group
C. CVE
D. None

QUESTION 54

When a user logs in via Captive Portal, their user data can be checked against:

A. Terminal Server Agent
B. Security Logs
C. XML API
D. Radius

QUESTION 55

A "Continue" action can be configured on the given Security Profiles:
A. URL Filtering, File Blocking, and Data Filtering
B. URL Filtering
C. URL Filtering and Antivirus
D. URL Filtering and File Blocking

QUESTION 56

As the Palo Alto Networks administrator, you have facilitated Application Block pages. Onceward, some users do not accept web-based feedback for all denied applications. Why would this be?

A. Some users are accessing the Palo Alto Networks firewall through a virtual system that does not have Application Block pages facilitated.
B. Application Block Pages will only be displayed when Captive Portal is configured
C. Some Application ID's are set with a Session Timeout value that is too low.
D. Application Block Pages will only be displayed when users effort to access a denied web-based application.

QUESTION 57

Wildfire may be used for identifying which of the given kinds of traffic?

A. URL content
B. DHCP
C. DNS
D. Viruses

QUESTION 58

When Network Address Translation has been performed on traffic, Destination Zones in Security regulations must be based on:

A. Post-NAT addresses
B. The same zones used in the NAT regulations
C. Pre-NAT addresses
D. None of the above

QUESTION 59

In Active/Active HA environments, dismissal for the HA3 interface can be achieved by:

A. Configuring a corresponding HA4 interface
B. Configuring HA3 as an Aggregate Ethernet bundle
C. Configuring numerous HA3 interfaces
D. Configuring HA3 in a redundant group

QUESTION 60

An Outbound SSL forward-proxy decryption regulation cannot be formed using which type of zone?

A. Virtual Wire

B. Tap

C. L3

D. L2

QUESTION 61

When a Palo Alto Networks firewall is forwarding traffic through interfaces configured for L2 mode, security policies can be set to match on multicast IP addresses.

A. Correct

B. Incorrect

QUESTION 62

In an Anti-Virus profile, changing the action to "Block" for IMAP or POP decoders will result in the given:

A. The connection from the server will be reset

B. The Anti-virus profile will behave as if "Alert" had been specified for the action

C. The traffic will be dropped by the firewall

D. Error 541 being sent back to the server

QUESTION 63

Once configuring Captive Portal in Layer 3 mode, users in the Trust Zone are not receiving the Captive Portal verification page when they launch their web browsers. How can this be adjusted?

A. Make sure that all users in the Trust Zone are using NTLM-capable browsers
B. Activate "Response Pages" in the Interface Management Profile that is functional to the L3 Interface in the Trust Zone.
C. Confirm that Captive Portal Timeout value is not set below 2 seconds
D. Activate "Redirect " as the Mode type in the Captive Portal Settings

QUESTION 64

The "Deactivate Server Return Inspection" choice on a security profile:

A. Can only be configured in Tap Mode
B. Must only be facilitated on security policies letting traffic to a trusted server.
C. Does not perform higher-level inspection of traffic from the side that originated the TCP SYN packet
D. Only performs inspection of traffic from the side that originated the TCP SYN-ACK packet

QUESTION 65

A user makes a complaint that they are no longer able to access a needed work application once you have implemented vulnerability and anti-spyware profiles. The user's application uses a unique port. What is the most efficient way to permit the user access to this application?

A. Utilize an Application Override Regulation, referencing the custom port utilized by this application. Application Override regulations bypass all Layer 7 inspection, thereby letting access to this application.
B. In the Threat log, locate the event which is blocking access to the user's application and make a IP-based exemption for this user.
C. In the vulnerability and anti-spyware profiles, make an application exemption for the user's application.
D. Make a custom Security regulation for this user to access the needed application. Do not apply vulnerability and anti-spyware profiles to this regulation.

QUESTION 66

You'd like to schedule a firewall policy to only permit a certain application during a particular time of day. Where can this policy choice be configured?

A. Policies > Security > Service
B. Policies > Security > Choices
C. Policies > Security > Application
D. Policies > Security > Profile

QUESTION 67

What is the size limitation of files manually uploaded to WildFire?

A. Configurable up to 10 megabytes

B. Hard-coded at 10 megabytes

C. Hard-coded at 2 megabytes

D. Configurable up to 20 megabytes

QUESTION 68

Activating "Highlight Unused Regulations" in the Security policy window will:

A. Highlight all regulations that did not immediately match traffic.

B. Highlight all regulations that did not match traffic since the regulation was formed or since last reboot of the firewall.

C. Lets the administrator to troubleshoot regulations when a validation error occurs at the time of commit.

D. Permit the administrator to temporarily deactivate regulations that do not match traffic, for testing purposes.

QUESTION 69

When making a Security Policy to permit Facebook in PAN-OS 5.0, how can you be sure that no other web-browsing traffic is permitted?

A. Make sure that the Service column is defined as "application-default" for this security regulation. This will automatically include the implicit web-browsing application dependency.
B. Make a subsequent regulation which blocks all other traffic
C. When making the regulation, make sure that web-browsing is added to the same regulation. Both applications will be processed by the Security policy, letting only Facebook to be accessed. Any other applications can be permitted in subsequent regulations.
D. No other configuration is needed on the part of the administrator, since implicit application dependencies will be added automatically.

QUESTION 70

In PAN-OS 5.0, how is Wildfire facilitated?

A. Via the URL-Filtering "Continue" Action
B. Wildfire is automatically facilitated with a valid URL-Filtering license
C. A custom file blocking action should be facilitated for all PDF and PE type files
D. Via the "Forward" and "Continue and Forward" File-Blocking actions

QUESTION 71

When configuring Security regulations based on FQDN objects, which of the given reports are correct?

A. The firewall resolves the FQDN first when the policy is committed, and is refreshed each time Security regulations are evaluated.

B. The firewall resolves the FQDN first when the policy is committed, and is refreshed at TTL expiration. There is no limit on the number of IP addresses stored for each resolved FQDN.

C. In order to make FQDN-based objects, you need to manually define a list of associated IP. Up to 10 IP addresses can be configured for each FQDN entry.

D. The firewall resolves the FQDN first when the policy is committed, and is refreshed at TTL expiration. The resolution of this FQDN stores up to 10 different IP addresses.

QUESTION 72

When troubleshooting Phase 1 of an IPSec VPN tunnel, what location will have the most informative logs?

A. Responding side, Traffic Logs

B. Initiating side, Traffic Logs

C. Responding side, System Logs

D. Initiating side, System Logs

QUESTION 73

Configuring a pair of devices into an Active/Active HA pair offers support for:

A. Higher session count
B. Redundant Virtual Routers
C. Asymmetric routing environments
D. Lower fail-over times

QUESTION 74

Which of the Dynamic Updates listed below are issued on a daily basis?

A. Global Protect
B. URL Filtering
C. Antivirus
D. Applications and Threats

QUESTION 75

Select the implicit regulations enforced on traffic failing to match any user defined Security Policies:

A. Intra-zone traffic is denied
B. Inter-zone traffic is denied
C. Intra-zone traffic is permitted
D. Inter-zone traffic is permitted

QUESTION 76

Palo Alto Networks firewalls support the use of both Dynamic (built-in user roles) and Role-Based (customized user roles).

A. Correct
B. Incorrect

QUESTION 77

In PAN-OS 6.0, regulation numbers were introduced. Regulation Numbers are:

A. Dynamic numbers that refer to a security policy's order and are especially useful when filtering security policies by tags
B. Numbers referring to when the security policy was formed and do not have a bearing on the order of policy enforcement
C. Static numbers that should be manually re-numbered whenever a latest security policy is added

QUESTION 78

Which of the given is NOT a valid choice for built-in CLI access roles?

A. read/write
B. superusers
C. vsysadmin
D. deviceadmin

QUESTION 79

Which of the given objects cannot use User-ID as a match conditions?

A. Security Policies
B. QoS
C. Policy Based Forwarding
D. DoS Protection
E. None of the above

QUESTION 80

Wildfire may be used for identifying which of the given kinds of traffic?

A. Malware
B. DNS
C. DHCP
D. URL Content

QUESTION 81

What are two sources of data for determining if the firewall has been successful in communicating with an external User-ID Agent?

A. System Logs and the indicator light under the User-ID Agent settings in the firewall
B. There's only one location - System Logs
C. There's only one location - Traffic Logs
D. System Logs and indicator light on the chassis

QUESTION 82

Subsequent to the installation of latest licenses, the firewall should be rebooted

A. Correct
B. Incorrect

QUESTION 83

When an interface is in Tap mode and a policy action is set to block, the interface will send a TCP reset.

A. Correct
B. Incorrect

QUESTION 84

The "Drive-By Download" protection attribute, under File Blocking profiles in Content-ID, gives:

A. Password-protected access to specific file downloads, for authorized users augmented speed on the downloads of the permitted file kinds
B. Protection against unwanted downloads, by alerting the user with a response page indicating that file is going to be downloaded
C. The Administrator the ability to leverage Verification Profiles in order to protect against unwanted downloads

QUESTION 85

Which of the given would be a reason to use an XML API to communicate with a Palo Alto Networks firewall?

A. So that data can be pulled from other network resources for User-ID
B. To permit the firewall to push UserID data to a Network Access Control (NAC) device.
C. To permit sys logging of User ID events

QUESTION 86

Which link is used by an Active-Passive cluster to synchronize session data?

A. The Data Link
B. The Control Link
C. The Uplink
D. The Management Link

QUESTION 87

Which of the given describes the sequence of the Global Protect agent connecting to a Gateway?

A. The Agent connects to the Portal obtains a list of Gateways, and connects to the Gateway with the fastest SSL response time
B. The agent connects to the closest Gateway and sends the HIP report to the portal
C. The agent connects to the portal, obtains a list of gateways, and connects to the gateway with the fastest PING response time
D. The agent connects to the portal and randomly establishes a connection to the first accessible gateway

QUESTION 88

With IKE, each device is identified to the other by a Peer ID. In most cases, this is just the public IP address of the device. In situations where the public ID is not static, this value can be replaced with a domain name or other text value

A. Correct
B. Incorrect

QUESTION 89

When configuring a Decryption Policy, which of the given are accessible as corresponding conditions in a policy? (Select three.)

A. Source Zone
B. Source User
C. Service
D. URL-Group
E. Application

QUESTION 90

Which of the given are procedures HA clusters use to identify network outages?

A. Path and Link Monitoring
B. VR and VSys Monitors
C. Heartbeat and Session Monitors
D. Link and Session Monitors

QUESTION 91

As a Palo Alto Networks firewall administrator, you have made unwanted changes to the Candidate configuration. These changes may be undone by Device > Setup > Operations > Configuration Management>   and then what operation?

A. Revert to Running Configuration
B. Revert to last Saved Configuration
C. Load Configuration Version
D. Import Named Configuration Snapshot

QUESTION 92

When employing the BrightCloud URL filtering database in a Palo Alto Networks firewall, the order of evaluation within a profile is:

A. Block list, Custom Groups, Predefined groups, Dynamic URL filtering, Permit list, Cache files.
B. Block list, Permit list, Custom Groups, Cache files, Local URL DB file.
C. Block list, Custom Groups, Cache files, Predefined groups, Dynamic URL filtering, Permit list.
D. Dynamic URL filtering, Block list, Permit list, Cache files, Custom groups, Predefined groups.

QUESTION 93

When Destination Network Address Translation is being performed, the destination in the corresponding Security Policy Regulation must use:

A. The PostNAT destination zone and PostNAT IP address.
B. The PreNAT destination zone and PreNAT IP address.
C. The PreNAT destination zone and PostNAT IP address.
D. The PostNAT destination zone and PreNAT IP address.

QUESTION 94

Considering only the data in the snapshot above, answer the given question. Which applications will be permitted on their standard ports?

A. BitTorrent
B. Gnutella
C. Skype
D. SSH

QUESTION 95

When using Config Audit, the color yellow indicates which of the given?

A. A setting has been changed amid the two config files
B. A setting has been deleted from a config file.
C. A setting has been added to a config file
D. An invalid value has been used in a config file.

QUESTION 96

What will the user experience when trying to access a blocked hacking website through a translation service such as Google Translate or Bing Translator?

A. A "Blocked" page response when the URL filtering policy to block is enforced.
B. A "Success" page response when the site is successfully translated.
C. The browser will be redirected to the original website address.
D. An "HTTP Error 503 Service inaccessible" message.

QUESTION 97

Both SSL decryption and SSH decryption are deactivated by default.

A. Correct
B. Incorrect

QUESTION 98

Can numerous administrator accounts be configured on a single firewall?

A. Yes
B. No

QUESTION 99

Which of the given should be facilitated in order for UserID to operate?

A. Captive Portal Policies should be facilitated.
B. UserID should be facilitated for the source zone of the traffic that is to be identified.
C. Captive Portal should be facilitated.
D. Security Policies should have the UserID choice facilitated.

QUESTION 100

Which of the given is a routing protocol supported in a Palo Alto Networks firewall?

A. RIPv2
B. ISIS
C. IGRP
D. EIGRP

QUESTION 101

WildFire analyzes files to decide whether or not they are malicious. When doing so, WildFire will classify the file with an official verdict. This verdict is known as the WildFire Analysis verdict. Select the three accurate classifications as a result of this analysis and classification?

A. Benign
B. Adware
C. Spyware
D. Malware detection
E. Safeware
F. Grayware

QUESTION 102

Without a WildFire subscription, which of the given files can be submitted by the Firewall to the hosted WildFire virtualized sandbox?

A. PE files only
B. PDF files only
C. MS Office doc/docx, xls/xlsx, and ppt/pptx files only
D. PE and Java Applet (jar and class) only

ANSWERS

1. Correct Answer: A
2. Correct Answer: ABE
3. Correct Answer: D
4. Correct Answer: D
5. Correct Answer: B
6. Correct Answer: D
7. Correct Answer: A
8. Correct Answer: D
9. Correct Answer: A
10. Correct Answer: B
11. Correct Answer: B
12. Correct Answer: AB
13. Correct Answer: D
14. Correct Answer: C
15. Correct Answer: A
16. Correct Answer: A
17. Correct Answer: A
18. Correct Answer: A
19. Correct Answer: C
20. Correct Answer: A
21. Correct Answer: A
22. Correct Answer: A
23. Correct Answer: A
24. Correct Answer: A
25. Correct Answer: BD
26. Correct Answer: A
27. Correct Answer: A
28. Correct Answer: D
29. Correct Answer: A
30. Correct Answer: A
31. Correct Answer: A
32. Correct Answer: A
33. Correct Answer: A
34. Correct Answer: B
35. Correct Answer: A
36. Correct Answer: D
37. Correct Answer: A
38. Correct Answer: D
39. Correct Answer: D

40. Correct Answer: D
41. Correct Answer: A
42. Correct Answer: D
43. Correct Answer: D
44. Correct Answer: D
45. Correct Answer: D
46. Correct Answer: A
47. Correct Answer: A
48. Correct Answer: C
49. Correct Answer: B
50. Correct Answer: D
51. Correct Answer: D
52. Correct Answer: D
53. Correct Answer: D
54. Correct Answer: D
55. Correct Answer: D
56. Correct Answer: D
57. Correct Answer: D
58. Correct Answer: A
59. Correct Answer: B
60. Correct Answer: A
61. Correct Answer: B
62. Correct Answer: B
63. Correct Answer: AB
64. Correct Answer: B
65. Correct Answer: B
66. Correct Answer: D
67. Correct Answer: A
68. Correct Answer: B
69. Correct Answer: D
70. Correct Answer: A
71. Correct Answer: C
72. Correct Answer: C
73. Correct Answer: B
74. Correct Answer: BC
75. Correct Answer: BC
76. Correct Answer: A
77. Correct Answer: A
78. Correct Answer: A
79. Correct Answer: E
80. Correct Answer: A
81. Correct Answer: A
82. Correct Answer: B

83. Correct Answer: B
84. Correct Answer: C
85. Correct Answer: B
86. Correct Answer: A
87. Correct Answer: A
88. Correct Answer: A
89. Correct Answer: ABD
90. Correct Answer: A
91. Correct Answer: A
92. Correct Answer: A
93. Correct Answer: D
94. Correct Answer: AD
95. Correct Answer: A
96. Correct Answer: A
97. Correct Answer: A
98. Correct Answer: A
99. Correct Answer: B
100.   Correct Answer: A
101.   Correct Answer: ADF
102.   Correct Answer: C